I0606084

Little People, **BIG DREAMS**™

WILLIAM SHAKESPEARE

Written by
Maria Isabel Sánchez Vegara

Illustrated by
Andrea Stegmaier

Frances Lincoln
Children's Books

Once upon a time, before movies or cartoons, there was a boy who enjoyed imagining stories of kings, lovers, ghosts, and fairies. His name was William, and he grew up in a busy little town in England called Stratford-upon-Avon.

At school, William spent his days learning an ancient language called Latin, and reading old stories. But what he loved most was watching the actors and performers who came to town. That's when his love for the stage truly began.

William was eighteen when he married a woman named Anne. Their first child, Susanna, was born soon after. Two years later came the twins, Hamnet and Judith, just as William's dreams began reaching far beyond his small town.

Hoping to start acting or—even better—writing, William moved to London. He could hardly imagine that he would become a successful actor and be celebrated as the writer of a famous play called *Henry VI*.

Not long after he arrived in the big city, many people began to get sick from a terrible illness called the plague. Theaters closed, and although William had already written several plays, he turned to poetry—using beautiful words and rhymes.

Bid me discourse I will enchant thine ear

When the theaters opened again, William wrote *Romeo and Juliet*, one of the greatest romances of all time . . .

. . . and *A Midsummer Night's Dream*, a comedy full of fairies, love mix-ups, and happy endings. It made people laugh!

But the laughter turned into sadness when one of his children, Hamnet, got sick and passed away. From that day on, William understood the joys and sorrows of life more than ever. He poured all these feelings into his writing.

Many believe William wrote *Hamlet*, one of his most famous works, while thinking of his son. In this story, a sad prince doesn't know what to do with all the pain in his heart. He asks a big question about life: "To be or not to be?"

The story was performed at London's Globe—a big, round theater with no roof that William had helped build. Everyone, from the noisy fans at the front to the noble guests in the balconies, fell silent during the sad scene.

Then came *Othello, King Lear,* and *Macbeth*—powerful stories full of big feelings, like jealousy, anger, and fear. William's words helped people understand what can happen when we let these emotions grow out of control.

King Lear
Macbeth

Whether funny, sad, brave, or confused, his characters felt so real that they stuck in people's minds. William used rich rhythms and clever words in his stories. He even made up phrases we still use today, like "in a pickle" or "heart of gold."

When William retired, he moved back to Stratford-upon-Avon to live a quiet life. But his stories kept shining in brand-new ways. For hundreds of years, people of all ages have lined up to see plays, movies, and musicals inspired by his words.

WEST SIDE STORY
WEST SIDE STORY
THE LION KING
10 things I hate about you

And still today, little William's voice speaks to the heart about love, fear, hope, and the big things we all wonder about.

That's why he's remembered as one of the greatest storytellers the world has ever known.

WILLIAM SHAKESPEARE

(Born 1564 – Died c. 1616)

c. 1610

c. 1610

William Shakespeare was born over 450 years ago in Tudor England. Because he lived so long ago, there are lots of things we don't know for certain about his life, including what he looked like! All the portraits you see above are thought to be of Shakespeare, but nobody knows for sure. Shakespeare grew up in a well-off family in Stratford-upon-Avon, where his father was a glove-maker. When he was eighteen, he married Anne Hathaway. They soon had a daughter, Susanna, followed in 1585 by twins called Hamnet and Judith. What Shakespeare did over the next seven years is a mystery. But by 1592, he was working in London as an actor and playwright, and was a rising star. In 1592–93, the plague swept through the city, killing more than one-tenth of the population. Theaters were forced

1616 – 1623

1623

to close, but Shakespeare kept busy writing poetry. When they reopened, he joined a new acting company called The Lord Chamberlain's Men. Over the next twenty years, he wrote over thirty plays, and became wealthy and famous. Many of his plays were performed at The Globe, a theater he helped build in 1599. There were exciting history plays (such as *Julius Caesar*), fun comedies (such as *Much Ado About Nothing*), and powerful tragedies (such as *Hamlet*). All dealt with big ideas and emotions that everyone could relate to, like love, jealousy, betrayal, ambition, and grief. In around 1611 Shakespeare returned to live in Stratford-upon-Avon. He died five years later, at age fifty-two. He is remembered as one of the greatest writers of all time.

Want to find out more about **William Shakespeare?**

Have a read of this great book:

Shakespeare (DK Eyewitness) by Peter Chrisp

If you visit London, England, you can go to The Globe.

Original idea of the series by Maria Isabel Sánchez Vegara, published by Alba Editorial, S.L.U
"Little People, BIG DREAMS" and "Pequeña & Grande" are trademarks of
Alba Editorial S.L.U. and/or Beautifool Couple S.L.
First Published in the US in 2026 by Frances Lincoln Children's Books, an imprint of The Quarto Group.
Quarto Boston North Shore, 100 Cummings Center, Suite 265D, Beverly, MA 01915, USA
Tel: +1 978-282-9590 **www.Quarto.com**
EEA Representation, WTS Tax d.o.o., Žanova ulica 3, 4000 Kranj, Slovenia. www.wts-tax.si

ISBN 978-1-80570-167-5
Set in Futura BT.

Published by Juliet Matthews · Designed by Sasha Moxon, Izzy Bowman, and Karissa Santos
Edited by Lucy Menzies and Claire Grace · Editorial management by Izzie Hewitt
Production by Robin Boothroyd
Manufactured in Shanghai , China CC112025
1 3 5 7 9 8 6 4 2

Photographic acknowledgements (pages 28-29, from left to right): 1. The Chandos Portrait, oil on canvas, attributed to John Taylor, c. 1610. 2. The "Cobbe Portrait," thought to be the only portrait of William Shakespeare painted during his lifetime. (Photo by VCG Wilson/Corbis via Getty Images.) 3. A bust of English playwright William Shakespeare in The Holy Trinity Church, Stratford-upon-Avon, Warwickshire. (Photo by RDImages/Epics/Getty Images.) 4. Portrait of William Shakespeare from the title page of the First Folio of Shakespeare's plays; copper engraving by Martin Droeshout, 1623. One of the earliest portraits of Shakespeare. (Photo by GraphicaArtis/Getty Images.)

Collect the *Little People,* **BIG DREAMS**™ series:

NELSON MANDELA | PABLO PICASSO | AMANDA GORMAN | GLORIA STEINEM | FLORENCE NIGHTINGALE | HARRY HOUDINI | J.R.R. TOLKIEN | ELVIS PRESLEY | NEIL ARMSTRONG

ALEXANDER VON HUMBOLDT | NIKOLA TESLA | WILMA MANKILLER | MARCUS RASHFORD | LAVERNE COX | MAE JEMISON | DWAYNE JOHNSON | HELEN KELLER | ANNA PAVLOVA

QUEEN ELIZABETH | TERRY FOX | HEDY LAMARR | SHAKIRA | FREDDIE MERCURY | LEWIS HAMILTON | LOUIS PASTEUR | PRINCESS DIANA | DAVID HOCKNEY

VANESSA NAKATE | OLIVE MORRIS | KING CHARLES | MOZART | STEVE IRWIN | JÜRGEN KLOPP | LEO MESSI | SALLY RIDE | TENZING NORGAY

KYLIE MINOGUE | BEYONCÉ | TAYLOR SWIFT | RAFA NADAL | USAIN BOLT | SIMONE BILES | STAN LEE | LEONARD COHEN | VINCENT VAN GOGH

MARY KOM | SALVADOR DALÍ | ANTOINE DE SAINT-EXUPÉRY | DAVID BECKHAM | KATHERINE JOHNSON | PATRICK MAHOMES | YAYOI KUSAMA | ROALD DAHL | HARRY STYLES

WILLIAM KAMKWAMBA | MARY EARPS | YVES SAINT LAURENT | BOB MARLEY | VIRGINIA WOOLF | LUDWIG VAN BEETHOVEN | LOUIS BRAILLE

STEVEN SPIELBERG | CHRIS HOY | MIKAELA SHIFFRIN | BEATRIX POTTER | RIHANNA | WILLIAM SHAKESPEARE

Scan the QR code for free activit
sheets, teachers' notes and more
information about the series at
www.littlepeoplebigdreams.com